This journal

belongs to

Date

· ·

- [ ]
- [ ]
- [ ]
- [ ]
- [ ]
- [ ]
- [ ]
- [ ]
- [ ]
- [ ]
- [ ]
- [ ]
- [ ]
- [ ]
- [ ]
- [ ]

Date

. . . .

Date

Date

· · · · · · · · · · · · · · · · · · · ·

Date

....

Date

. . . .

Date

Date

....

Date

Date

Date

Date

· ·

Date

Date

. . . .

Date

. . . .

Date

. . . .

Date

Date

. . . .

Date

Date

. . . .

Date

....

Date

Date

Date

Date

· ·

Date

....

Date

. . . .

Date

Date

· ·

☐ ____ ☐
☐ ____ ☐
☐ ____ ☐
☐ ____ ☐
☐ ____ ☐
☐ ____ ☐
☐ ____ ☐
☐ ____ ☐
☐ ____ ☐
☐ ____ ☐
☐ ____ ☐
☐ ____ ☐
☐ ____ ☐
☐ ____ ☐
☐ ____ ☐
☐ ____ ☐

Date

....

Date

Date

. . . .

Date

· ·

Date

. . . .

Date

. . . .

- [ ]
- [ ]
- [ ]
- [ ]
- [ ]
- [ ]
- [ ]
- [ ]
- [ ]
- [ ]
- [ ]
- [ ]
- [ ]
- [ ]
- [ ]
- [ ]

Date

Date

....

Date

· ·

☐ ____ ☐
☐ ____ ☐
☐ ____ ☐
☐ ____ ☐
☐ ____ ☐
☐ ____ ☐
☐ ____ ☐
☐ ____ ☐
☐ ____ ☐
☐ ____ ☐
☐ ____ ☐
☐ ____ ☐
☐ ____ ☐
☐ ____ ☐
☐ ____ ☐

Date

- [ ]
- [ ]
- [ ]
- [ ]
- [ ]
- [ ]
- [ ]
- [ ]
- [ ]
- [ ]
- [ ]
- [ ]
- [ ]
- [ ]
- [ ]
- [ ]

Date

. . . .

Date

Date

....

Date

Date

Date

Date

· ·

Date

Date

Date

Date

· ·

Date

Date

· · · · · · · · · · · · · · · · · · · ·

Date

Date

Date

Date

Date

Date

· ·

Date

....

Date

· ·

Date

· ·

Date

Date

Date

. . . .

Date

....

Date

· ·

Date

Date

Date

· ·

- ☐ ____ ☐
- ☐ ____ ☐
- ☐ ____ ☐
- ☐ ____ ☐
- ☐ ____ ☐
- ☐ ____ ☐
- ☐ ____ ☐
- ☐ ____ ☐
- ☐ ____ ☐
- ☐ ____ ☐
- ☐ ____ ☐
- ☐ ____ ☐
- ☐ ____ ☐
- ☐ ____ ☐
- ☐ ____ ☐

Date

· · · · · · · · · · · · · · · · · · · ·

- [ ]
- [ ]
- [ ]
- [ ]
- [ ]
- [ ]
- [ ]
- [ ]
- [ ]
- [ ]
- [ ]
- [ ]
- [ ]
- [ ]
- [ ]
- [ ]

Date

Date

....

Date

Date

Date

· ·

Date

....

Date

....

Date

. . . .

Date

Date

Date

Date

· ·

Date

· ·

Date

· ·

Date

Date

Date

. . . .

Date

....

Date

. . . .

Date

Date

Date

. . . .

Date

Date

. . . .

- [ ]
- [ ]
- [ ]
- [ ]
- [ ]
- [ ]
- [ ]
- [ ]
- [ ]
- [ ]
- [ ]
- [ ]
- [ ]
- [ ]
- [ ]

Date

Date

· ·

Date

· · · · · · · · · · · · · · · · · · · ·

Date

· · · · · · · · · · · · · · · · · · · ·

Date

Date

Date

....

Date

Date

Date

. . . .

Date

··

Date

. . . .

- ☐
- ☐
- ☐
- ☐
- ☐
- ☐
- ☐
- ☐
- ☐
- ☐
- ☐
- ☐
- ☐
- ☐
- ☐

Date

Date

. . . .

Date

Date

Date

Date

Date

Date

# Date

....

Date

....

Date

· ·

Date

· ·

Date

· ·

Date

· ·

Date

· ·

Date

· ·

Date

· ·

Date

. . . .

Date

Date

Date

Date

. . . .

Date

Date

Date

Date

· ·

Date

· ·

- [ ]
- [ ]
- [ ]
- [ ]
- [ ]
- [ ]
- [ ]
- [ ]
- [ ]
- [ ]
- [ ]
- [ ]
- [ ]
- [ ]
- [ ]
- [ ]

Date

Date

Date

. . . .

Date

....

Date

· ·

Date

· ·

Date

....

Date

Date

Date

....

Date

Date

....

☐ ___________________________________ ☐

☐ ___________________________________ ☐

☐ ___________________________________ ☐

☐ ___________________________________ ☐

☐ ___________________________________ ☐

☐ ___________________________________ ☐

☐ ___________________________________ ☐

☐ ___________________________________ ☐

☐ ___________________________________ ☐

☐ ___________________________________ ☐

☐ ___________________________________ ☐

☐ ___________________________________ ☐

☐ ___________________________________ ☐

☐ ___________________________________ ☐

☐ ___________________________________ ☐

Date

· · · · · · · · · · · · · · · · · · · ·

Thank you.

We hope you enjoyed our journal.

As a small family company, your feedback is very important to us.

Please let us know how you like our journal at:

mollymcluke@gmail.com